TH

Cal

Also by Caleb Parkin

This Fruiting Body   (Nine Arches Press, 2021)

Wasted Rainbow   (tall-lighthouse, 2021)

ISBN: 978-1-915079-44-2

The author has asserted their right to be identified as the author of this Work in accordance with the Copyright, Designs and Patents Act 1988

Cover designed by Aaron Kent

Edited and typeset by Aaron Kent

Broken Sleep Books Ltd
Rhydwen,
Talgarreg,
SA44 4HB
Wales

Contents

The Coin

Caleb Parkin

For Sandy
Betty
and Joy

The Coin

All women become like their mothers.
That is their tragedy. No man does. That is his.
— Oscar Wilde

Nevertheless, I breeze through the world's emporia, equipped
with titbits of finely diced life, whiffled under servers' noses:
hummingbird-raptor, hunter of chatter. I flit between tills,
hands not reflected in their counters. My mother's grip
lingers on receipts like a lifejacket, longing to thumb-flick

a crumb, a morsel, bait. Now, I go into the cut-price
smiles of chemists and butchers with intent:
conjure snippets with overwrought gestures,
offer a coin to every stranger,
daring them to flip it.

she is the mountain & the mountain is moving

before mum un-migrates we go up up up
to *La Gourette*   via hairpins grassicles
icicles   alpine eaves shrouded in fog
& static   our ears pop three times
from her talking   about the
telecommunications company
& his *Arab French-speaking*
with her *Anglo French-speaking*
(*grave* accents   acute parentheses)
all her stories are about victory
the ways she won against Orange
against the guests   against
a world uninterested in stopping
to help   against the past   against
husbands or those who came after
she opts out of sledging   then films
her thumb as we fill our mouths
with powder   we heft up the hill
dig fists into the crunching depths
and every hour she asks if we'd like
matryoshka dolls   ski boots
handknitted blankets from photos
of baby brothers   before it all gets
boxed or chucked   or boxed for
another ten years   she sobs
about leaving the rotavator   the rain
on the greening swimming pool   the time
a friend's baby died   & we are being
written into this chapter now   archived
in that Svalbard Global Seed Vault
mind of hers   as we leave I say
If anyone can- & she says *I know*

& her eyes   unmoveable   melt

learning to spell 'leukaemia'

every time that surprise
'u' and intrusive 'a'
something to do with blood

that *-ia* suffix says *medicine*
when it pricks your speech
and you will question why

and for whom you are
divulging it at all   when it
drips through pen

cylinders or down synapses
to jabbing fingers
you wonder each time

why blood goes rogue
when bones go wrong
how body doesn't know

when to finish a cell's story
and so we give it its own
container   this canker

that word staring back
like a newsreader faltering
as the autocue whirls

hating ferrets

comes from the canonical tale where a ferret bit into
the bone of mum's hand / as she tells it / that bastard
thing hung from her digit / blood rivulets along its
length / incisors embedded /as she reached for the
shotgun

one of those Elmer Fudd type double-barrelled
numbers / or so I imagine it / she aimed it point-
blank at the ferret / which for dramatic purposes /
I'm assuming was white

somehow she pulls that other arm back far enough
/ now Diana the Huntress with added Rambo / and
fires –

the rest is implied in silhouette / but likely included
a lot of cleaning up / both human and / to a differing
extent / ferret

Veronica

whose son calls my mum *Mummy Two*. Who
tracks up the driveway (that's more like a lane) in a Renault
Espace. Whose hair is pulled back in a bun high as her
Classic FM voice – *I can't help it darling, it's the schools
they sent me to –*

Who makes an impeccable Laura Ashley cocoon beneath
the flammable cottage roof. Whose right arm whisks very-
specifically-buttery scrambled egg, on a charred Aga top
and whose left arm, for the fifth time today, cordlessly stirs
a customer service line, *I wonder if you can help me?*

Who, seen from above, wanders out from under the
mouldering thatch, towards a broiling blue rectangle full of
whirlpools. Who criss-crosses between chicken shed roofs:
allegedly a poultry farmer. But even in a uniform of coarse
jumper, black leggings, chickenshit wellies and a layer of
grey Wolfhound-mohair, she reeks of glamour full of
feathers.

Whose kids are propped on surfaces everywhere, changing
in photos, paintings – *Christopher's neck got thicker and thicker,
sitting to sitting* – their names glossy, embossed reminders.

Who pauses by creak-twisting stairs, stares into the gold-leaf
frame, where player-in-chief Hamlet stares back, skull
in his hand, thinking of Mummy One.

Captain Kathryn Janeway's catchphrase, 'do it', never caught on

Mid-explanation of quantum paradox,
Captain Kathryn Janeway starts
peeling potatoes. Real ones, not those
replicated-to-molecular-perfection
or ready-to-roast ones. Throned in her
ready room, peeler set to kill, a starchy
hillock builds as she expounds
the finer points of the Prime Directive
to an imperious Seven of Nine.
She orders *battle stations, shields up*,
one hand giving the signal to fire,
the other beating Yorkshire pud batter.
It will have time to rest. Crisis averted.
On the holodeck, sparring intellectually
with a photonic Leonardo DaVinci,
she's also chopping carrots into batons.
And in the season finale, whilst navigating
the ethics of Kes's uncontrollable
adolescent telekinesis, just off-screen
Janeway is layering trifle sponges.

To the River Stour

some call you *S'toor*, like *poor*
and I thought this your proper
posher name because mum
pronounced you that way

others called you *St-our*, like *our*
and maybe that's your name
too as you wiggle like an idyll
on a National Trust postcard

through Essex-Suffolk floodplain
horizon   pinned on with spires
punctured by telephone masts
ears trained on each glottal stop

coppiced willows flank your banks
boaters meander as they squint
to find tributaries into Constable
gorgeous and serene so flat and yet

I longed for the wide mouth
of estuaries   the way they aren't
one thing or another   their brackish
manner   part-play   part-threat

Stour, St-oor, St-hour, you're a Site
of Special Scientific Pinterest
a keepnet for Nordic walkers
a cowpat for bluebottle tourists

and streams of gleaming Land
Rovers yearning for a blemish
a picture-perfect cream tea
on an English patina, cracking

designer socks

a tradition for several years
when on Christmas eve
mum carefully snipped
the plastic tags off each pair
from the pound shop
then artfully mismatched them

stripes disrupting spots
geometric with a festive clash

I forget which configuration
of family we were then
but all those socks got
tombola'd in the same
washing machine drum

and we'd spend all year
redesigning them

Good Friday in Mum's Shed

sifting hammerheads, flat-tired bikes,
boxes and boxes of fabric scraps.
We stand back, regard
all these categorized stacks
on the green lawn, and place
things with others in some way like them
and while we do, I recall
the casual way she said over dinner
last night that if this doesn't work

this time – she won't go through that
treatment again. And then busily, she
shows us more boxes of bargain fabrics,
some overgrown with embroidered flowers
and another printed with sprinting hares,
and we all head off to bed to dream
in frayed patchworks, slackening stitches.

Pianola

P-
u
n
c
h
e
d   on
            this
                  mobius mind are the dark thrash-
                                                    ing
chords from some s t a r k c o m p o s i t i o n but
no longer its name
                        lost somewhere in a black box
in what   Mum operatically called   *TheDrawingRoom*
a slapstick spectacular,   a Western Saloon.

Come: rest your   d-i-g-i-t-s on these keys
hook yourself up   to this
                        lacquered   machine
start to pe-
                  dal   fur-
                                    iously   or ten-tatively
depen-ding   on-these   ordered
                                          absences, holes
in yellowed scrolls:
                        this   music will
play   you   again, your strings
                              will t ---wang
back   & in   your   fing-ers   &   toes
your   feet   will   mark   out
        our home's   rhythm & you'll feel
just-   how-   loud   time-can-seem
just-   how-   worn   love-can-be

18

Tenner

Lugging Jan's wheelchair across brittle furrows
to the Suffolk Show gate, I dropped the note:
lost in that maze of field-parked estate cars,

all that potential for £1 per 100g sweets,
simulators, speed-restricted quad bikes,
or failing to hook a rubber duck –

lost, slipped from my pink shell-suit pocket.
Instead of the Queen's gaze – distant, paper-thin,
poised to be traded in – there were Jan's eyes,

just below my own. She looked back with such
bright compassion, through a face whose muscles
were slowly wasting. Straw scritted everywhere,

under Jan's slight feet, while she witnessed
all I had lost. And Mum said, *Don't worry love.*
We'll get you another one. We'll get you another.

While Mum Describes Her Side Effects

my sequin vest revolves in the machine
and messages ping from distant siblings.

We're all on a crash course in terminologies,
studying lymphocytes and subtexts, remotely.

A brother on WhatsApp jokes about stem
cells putting down carpets, before they select

wallpaper, making themselves at home.
As the vest revolves, the round door becomes

a glittering cross-section, a fabulation, a diagram
of her bones, something magic now inside them.

This numinous matter zapped from a donor,
swirling until the programme ends, our

mother emerging, fresh. In the meantime,
we're in Yorkshire, Madrid, adrift in time

zones: all of us trying to feel at home.

To an Uncle

whose funeral I missed for a writing retreat.
A death of quick symptoms, a lump
in the throat, fast progression and
far-off silence.
               The brother of my mum,
gone. No photos, barely a memory; a kinship
of genes, entangled code.
                        For years you'd simply
existed, unseen 'over east' among polytunnels
and driveways, routine solid as the postcode.

Unseen to me, embedded in road-veins, town-
clumps, on the ear of East Anglia; North Sea
grey on green, wheezing between us.

Wrabness

was it the warring wrasses
the swans' wan brawn
how we brothers nabbed crabs
swabbed from under catamarans

branflakes banned   only chips
geological slabs of buttered bread
we wren wraiths skittered furrows
between dust-smothered huts

their wooden slats dashed
in pristine beans of April hail
hitting thin sand-smudged panes
that looked across to that tower

as though Big Ben shed its
skin slid its way here to rear
over this estuary   how we saw
reflections in saltish grainy

Stour water could swear there
were others staring back up

Birdwatching in Stereo

When she felt at her worst
        Mum sat in the living room
merged with the sofa, stared
        through the patio doors
out to the neighbours' roofs
        where gulls bickered and built
on their tiled horizon.

> *Wrens don't complain they're diminutive*
> *don't question their wings or motives*
> *with only these flitting instants to live.*

On her lawn, the birdfeeder
        offered sunflower seeds,
a shallow bath, the silhouetted
        idea of a bird in metal:
a two-dimensional
        character, designed
to set an example.

> *The robins do not lack motivation*
> *as they flutter-crash on feeding stations*
> *eyeing which seed to take, which to shun.*

She said she'd watched
        for hours, unable
to busy herself with
        background knitting.
Those patio doors, a livestream
        out on activity, on life.

> *The magpies have come,*
> *don't care if you count them.*

Contains: Grandmothers

<Joy.gif>

Joy.clown hands pennies from rattan
seat to feed into iron Pierrot GULP
iron Pierrot GULP. <glitches back
back from action of giving
copper coin grows in palm
self-regenerated fortune-
teller / flipped conjuror
children = white rabbits>
query: what were you
really collecting?

Joy.hedgehogs1 hobbles garden path
descending on "hodgehegs" she half-
poisons w/ catfood cowmilk love
<a few little steps, side-lit by window
frames / breath archive slo-mo
steam train steam train steam train>
query: which of those hedge-
hogs was your favourite?

Joy.crumbs on that cross-country
railway sleeper table – sweeps
digestives licks finger pristine
pristine licks finger sweeps plate
clear white clear circle <crumbs grow
drift grow dusty edited digestives accum-
umulate accumulating each loop
plate fills filling first little cairn first
a sandcastle first whole sand-frame
filling fills sand-dune time-lapse
under tonnes that action of
finger to tongue to plate to finger ->
query: do I hold my cutlery
like you, or not at all?

\<Betty.gif>

`Betty.jigsaw` looks btwn window
& jigsaw jigsaw & window
puzzle beaming diagonal //
up to the net-curtain static.
\<edge-box of 1 0 0 0 – p i e c e r
complete - - - remainder of favoured
British village in rubble to be re-
assembled re-remembered
raised hand holds piece
w/bungalow window, a face
her face faintly visible - >

`Betty.cupboard` places two
mugs back in allotted spot
standard spot in white
Formica. \<clip self-edits
shorter
to mugs X 1
colours = muted>

`Betty.BritishLegion` encased
beneath corrugated woodlouse
roof smoke roof-height corrugated
chat \<pushes buttons on the
pushes fruit machine eyes
lining up / aligning with dials:
same same same
HOLD HOLD it starts
to Mobius strip: frame
hazes, mists & hazes
everything lifts
shifts everything
orange orange oranges
become tethered red planets

of buoys / vines on the wall lift
bottom to top great swipes
curlicue & sway kelp curlicue &
Betty's cast-iron loafers
press pressed pressing
please HOLD HOLD

90th

Somebody pops to *Big Tesco* for more ingredients
for divorce; we check the back of the fridge for

different-flavoured cures for cancer. We wheel
our best stainless-steel selves out into the hall,

where floral dresses have become swampy
with pitcher plant, Venus flytraps that gnash

over gingham-lashed sandwiches. Teacups
clash with three-tiered home-drilled cake-stands.

The old waggle their crockery with pursed lips, binbags
filling inexorably, while candles ignite the fire alarm.

Through the serving hatch, witness at least a hundred
greatgrandchildren process, lost in a forest of crutches:

on each child's head, a geranium teeters, an offering.

Leonard

i.m. Joy

Gran claimed she'd found another lion
identical to her Leonard, right down to
his wonky tail – *So you can have him*,
she said, throned in sagging wicker,
bestowing the fluffy yellow hunter
like a knighthood. With a side-eye
that acknowledged what they both
understood: there was only
ever one Leonard to be gifted.

*

That summer, Leonard got hoisted
up a flagpole; *Rikki-Tikki-Tavi* sat in
a khaki coven at the mouth of their tent.
The men claimed this casual sacrifice
was in honour of a sports team, named
The Lions. That night, a languid
claw ripped a second zip, right by
Bagheera's nose: the breeze Leonard's
name, whispered on fetid breath.

dressing room

mum as make-up artist
powders the blank space where
my waking face would be

which scene – the one
where I perform the operation
on the dog? the one with
the teeth? are the SFX team
prepped for the flood retakes?
is my stunt-double standing by
for the green screen fight scene
with my childhood friend's mother?

mum   the make-up artist   becomes
a drifting grin   an opiate wisp

is it the one where my character
carries models of an owl in one hand
and a crane in the other? where i
dance flamenco on a stack of
fractured plastic garden chairs?

she evaporates in two cold drafts
at my collarbones   my dressing gown
slumps   down   through the floor

In the Bungalow

after Jane Kenyon
i.m. Betty

She is like the biscuit tin
whose lid has been lifted
so many times, her landscape
design is blizzarding away.

She wants to offer you her last
pink wafer, custard cream, but has
only rich teas to match the pale brew
of her breath, her skimmed nights.

See how we are mirrored in the base
of her, scattered amongst the crumbs.

How Am I Driving?

My hands rest on their pinkies
as mum's do, driving the DNA
spiral of this NCP ramp,
handling these corners
like high-hedged lanes,
changing gears and topics
without a glance, sometimes
on the hands-free – and all
effortlessly at once. Now,
without fear, any particular
concentration, I follow these arrows
nimbly, knowing just where my
bumpers and corners are, how
my gears align with each slope.

Two Tablespoonfuls

she asked the Crem for. Or it might have been, *two tablespoons*, the former being an official measurement, rather than an informal tag or nickname: *table-spoon, tablespoon, tablespoonful, Nanna, Mama*. Table-spoons being part of the profusion of 18th-century spoons: *mustard-spoon, salt-spoon, coffee-spoon, half-spoon, step-spoon*.

She didn't ask for the equivalent 29.6 millilitres: how do you measure that out from the cremulator? Can you ask whether it's more demerara or caster? Just two tablespoons from the interred mass; a sprinkle of grey icing on an earthy chocolate cake. Pot a rose up on top, though, and watch it wither.

Not dessertspoons, soupspoons. Both lack gravity. No, she requires the best spoon / best-spoon / bestspoon. The Sunday roast spoon: two slices of pale meat, peas unpodded, carrots like worn-out suns. The favourite spoon.

Not three teaspoonfuls, the ten-a-penny, clink-in-the-cutlery-drawer kind used to stir sugar into wan tea. *Two tablespoons* – for serving or eating. Not half a fluid ounce, because this was not fluid, but more flour, self-raising.

Were they for a diamond, a pendant, to be mounted on a glinting sceptre? Or who's to say they wouldn't end up funnelled, bottled, nestled in the spice rack, between *Marjoram* and *Nutmeg*?

It used to be that you carried your own spoon around to every table: your personal spoon. Not the stainless-steel municipal free-for-all of shared spoons, rows and rows of them, names taking and sloughing off hyphens: *grapefruit-spoon, slotted spoon, sugar-spoon, love spoon*.

Two tablespoons. The table and the spoon, joined for decades, centuries, by a hyphen, until they became a measure in themselves. Those two full spoons she took, then fired that hyphen - a dart into the bullseye, missile into the sun.

The Pattern

MY MOTHER MADE ME A HOMOSEXUAL.
If I gave her the wool, would she make me one too?
— Anon. Graffiti, London, c. 1978

If she could, she'd knit you a boyfriend or a balaclava.
She'd knit you a softer day, a longer year – a macramé
life with a looser weave; a fingerless glove or new lover;
a man or a mansion. If she could. But she'll knit

anyway, from any old yarn and turn it into
its opposite. Through endless TV murders,
those needles banish death, their clickety-
clacketing wishes summon cosy multiverses.

And even though the twine might get
slightly too tight, the ends slightly frayed,
she'll knit with her every last synapse.
Rest is off the table, until it's all made

wearable, bearable, understood.
If you've got the will
and she's got the wool,
then she would.

Acknowledgements

Thanks to the editors of the following publications, where versions of some of these poems appeared: *Anthropocene, Dust, Finished Creatures, Raceme.*

'To the River Stour' was shortlisted in the Gingko Ecopoetry Prize AONB Best Poem of Landscape and appeared in its anthology.

'Two Tablespoonfuls' was longlisted in the Keats-Shelley Prize 2022 on the theme of 'Elegy'.

With huge thanks to the HOURS critique group, whose commitment and critiques I value immensely.

To Simon Maddrell, for splendid pedantry in looking at this manuscript in its final stages: it is so much better for it, thank you.

For Wendy Pratt's thoughtful input on earlier versions of a number of these poems.

With thanks, as ever, to all my families, biological, chosen, more-than-human: to Paul and Scruffs; my urban family; to sangha; to my vast and unruly family shrub – especially all the matriarchs.

LAY OUT YOUR UNREST

Lightning Source UK Ltd.
Milton Keynes UK
UKHW010717081222
413589UK00006B/168